Cookie Caper

by Eduardo Perez
illustrated by Jayoung Cho

HOUGHTON MIFFLIN   BOSTON

PHOTOGRAPHY CREDITS
Cover © MetaCreations/Kai Power Photos; **1** © MetaCreations/Kai Power Photos

Copyright © by Houghton Mifflin Company. All rights reserved.

No part of this work may be reproduced or transmitted in any form or by any means, electronic or mechanical, including photocopying or recording, or by any information storage or retrieval system without the prior written permission of Houghton Mifflin Company unless such copying is expressly permitted by federal copyright law. Address inquiries to School Permissions, Houghton Mifflin Company, 222 Berkeley Street, Boston, MA 02116.

Printed in China

ISBN 10: 0-618-89972-3
ISBN 13: 978-0-618-89972-2

13 14 15 16 17 0940 20 19 18 17 16

4500590856

When my sister and I got home from school, we smelled freshly baked cookies. We patted Taffy and went right into the kitchen.

"We're so lucky," said Carly. "Let's share them."
"Sure, Carly. But how do we make it fair?"
"Just divide. That's when you split things into equal groups."

Read·Think·Write How many cookies do they each get?

I looked down at the cookies and the answer was right there. "That's easy. There are five cookies for you and five cookies for me."

"There you go, Corey. You just divided!"

We were just going to eat our cookies when my friends Trevor, Lisa, and Carlos rang the bell.
Now we had 10 cookies for five people.

Read·Think·Write How could they divide the cookies fairly for five people?

It wasn't a problem. I looked at the cookies and the answer was right there. "Each person gets two cookies." I said.

"You are a total math whiz," said Trevor. "Now, can we please eat the cookies before Taffy does?"

The bell rang AGAIN! This time it was my aunt, my uncle, and my triplet cousins. Yikes! Now there were ten people.

Read·Think·Write Now how many cookies does each person get?

I didn't need to look at the cookies this time. I knew there were ten cookies for ten people.

"Each person gets one cookie," I said. "I hope the doorbell doesn't ring again!"

We all looked at the door and listened. Nobody rang the bell.

"Finally! Let's eat!" I said. Everyone took a bite.

I looked at Taffy's sad eyes. "Poor dog! He wants a cookie, too."

"Hold on Taffy, here's your very own cookie!"

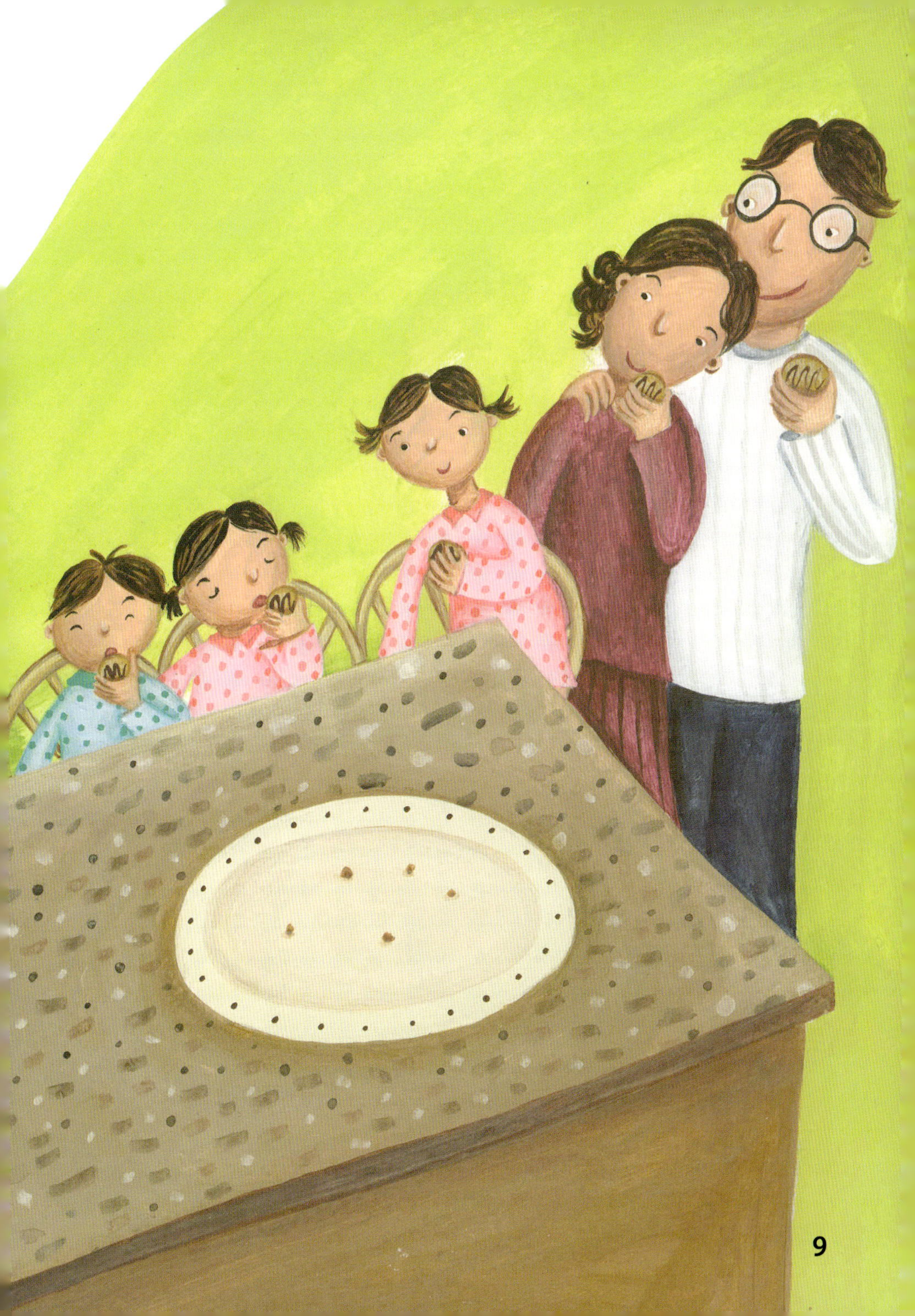

At last everyone had a cookie. There sure was a lot of crunching going on in the kitchen.

Responding

Math Concepts

Use paper clips or counters to help you answer these questions.

1. Suppose Taffy ate two of the ten cookies before Corey could stop her. How many cookies would Corey and Carly each get?
2. Suppose there were 20 cookies for five people. How many cookies would each person get?
3. What if just Carly and Corey were sharing 20 cookies? How many would each get?

Activity

Follow Directions, Oral and Written

You will need:
- One or more friends
- 10 "cookies" per player (this can be any object, like counters or even circles of construction paper that you decorate to look like cookies)

continued

Responding continued

- Number cards (or small pieces of paper). To start, make 4 number cards. Print one of the following numbers on each card: 1, 2, 5, 10.

To Play:
- Place the number cards face-down on the table and mix them up.
- Each player sits in front of their cookies.
- One player turns over a number card. If 2 is turned over, the player says "Cookie party for two."
- Each player makes equal piles for two people. See how quickly you can place the right number of cookies in each pile.
- Start over again! Have fun!